WILLIAM BOLCOM
PIANO CONCERTO
for Piano and Large Orchestra

reduction for 2 pianos/4 hands

Commissioned by the Seattle Symphony, Milton Katims, Conductor
Premiered by same with William Bolcom at the piano, March 8, 1976

RECORDED ON:

Vox Classics #7509 – "Bolcom/Adler Works for Piano and Flute"
William Bolcom, piano, Rochester Philharmonic Orchestra, Sydney Hodkinson, conductor

and

Hyperion CDA67170
Marc-André Hamelin, piano, The Ulster Orchestra, Dmitry Sitkovetsky, conductor

Full score and parts on rental from:
Theodore Presser Company
588 North Gulph Road
King of Prussia, PA 19406

EDWARD B.
MARKS MUSIC
COMPANY

EXCLUSIVELY DISTRIBUTED BY
HAL•LEONARD®
CORPORATION
7777 W. BLUEMOUND RD. P.O. BOX 13819 MILWAUKEE, WI 53213

Dédié à la mémoire de mon grand maître,
Darius Milhaud

PIANO CONCERTO

Duration: approx. 25'

WILLIAM BOLCOM
(1975-1976)
[Orchestral reduction (2nd Piano)
by the composer]

GLOSSARY:

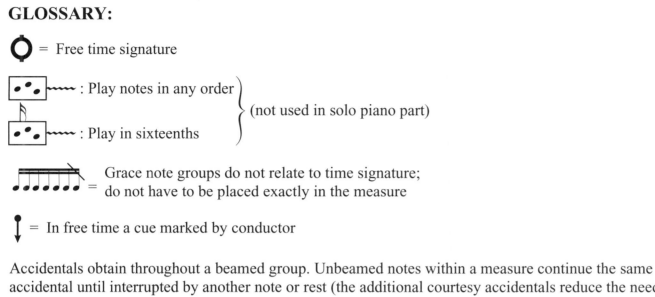

= Free time signature

: Play notes in any order } (not used in solo piano part)

: Play in sixteenths

= Grace note groups do not relate to time signature;
do not have to be placed exactly in the measure

= In free time a cue marked by conductor

Accidentals obtain throughout a beamed group. Unbeamed notes within a measure continue the same accidental until interrupted by another note or rest (the additional courtesy accidentals reduce the need to return the eye to the beginning of the measure). In music with key signatures, traditional rules apply.

I. Andante spianato - Allegro

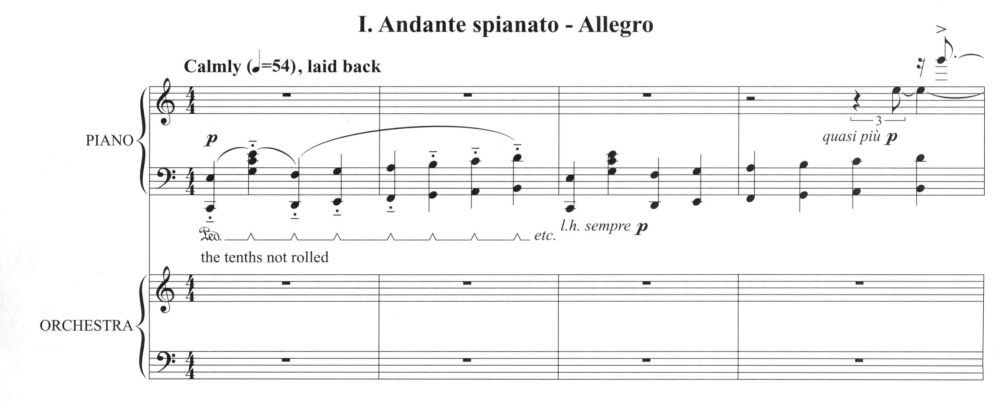

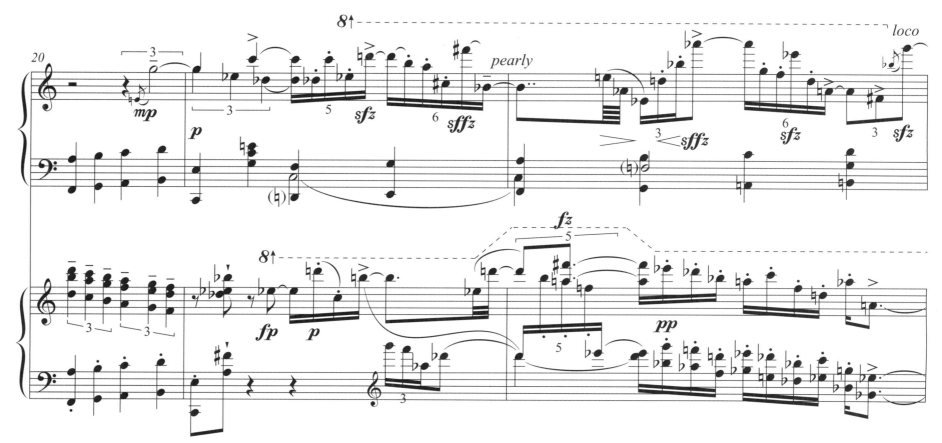

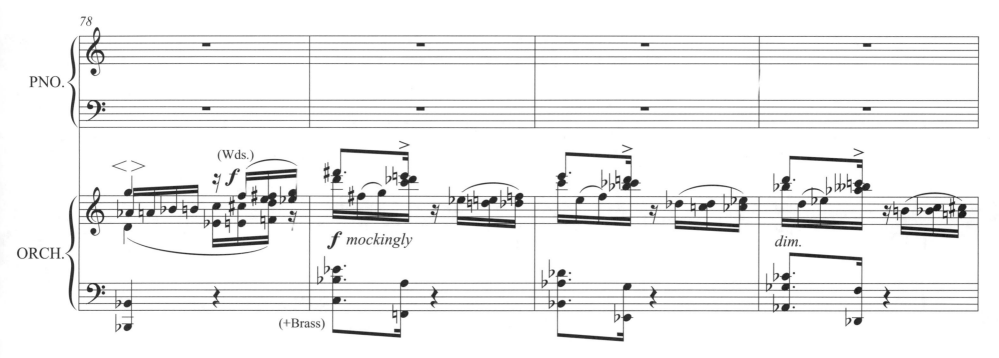

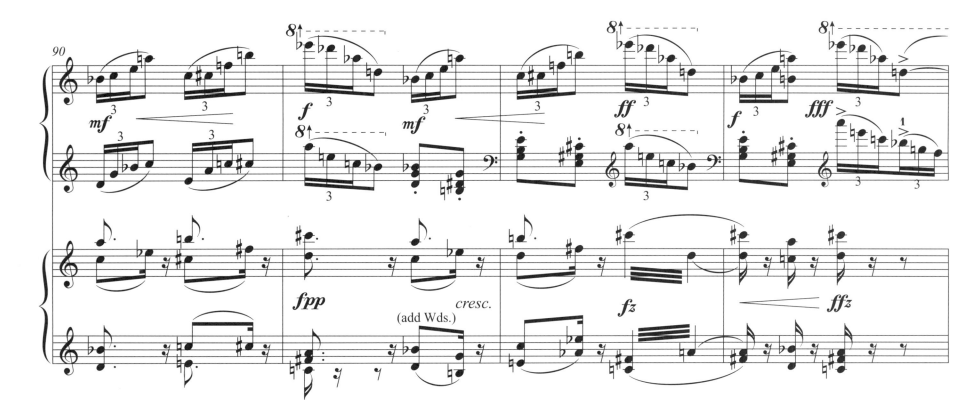

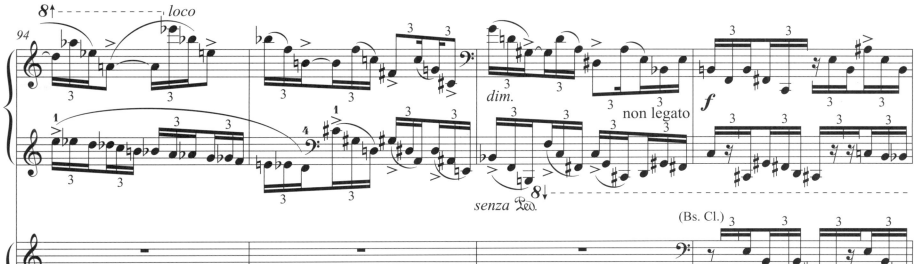

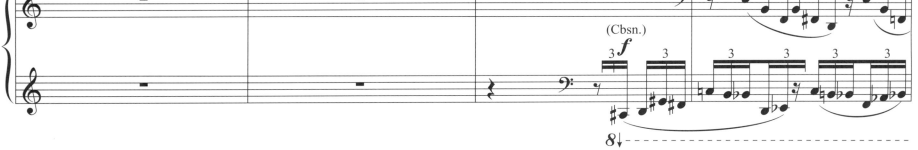

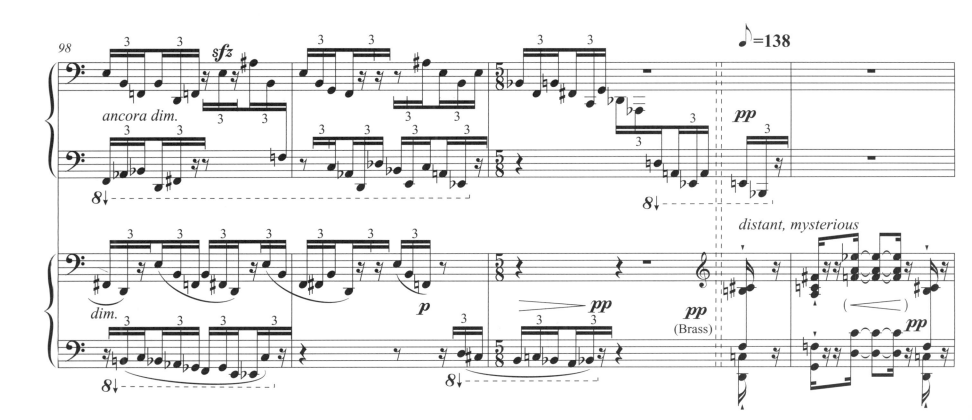

Piano harmonics:
touch string with right-hand
finger so that diamond note
sounds (node is generally
found just behind damper)

* These piano harmonics can be spread out further into the following measures *ad libitum*.

* These harmonics can be begun several measures earlier and spread out.

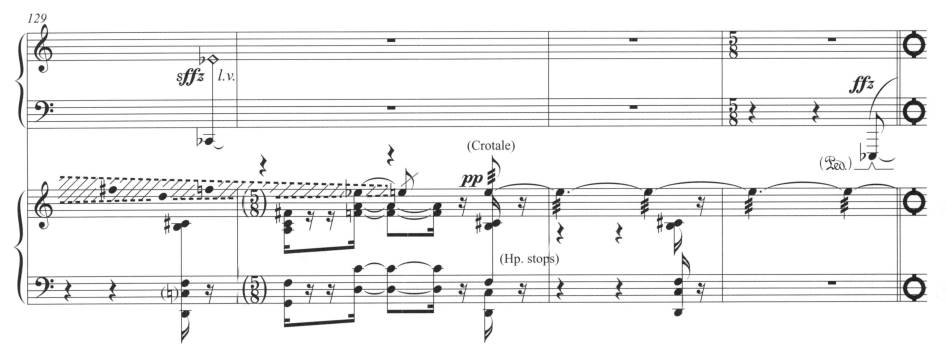

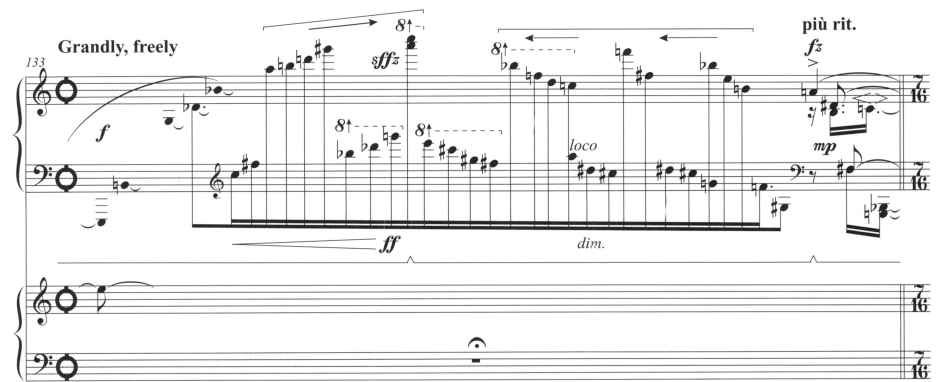

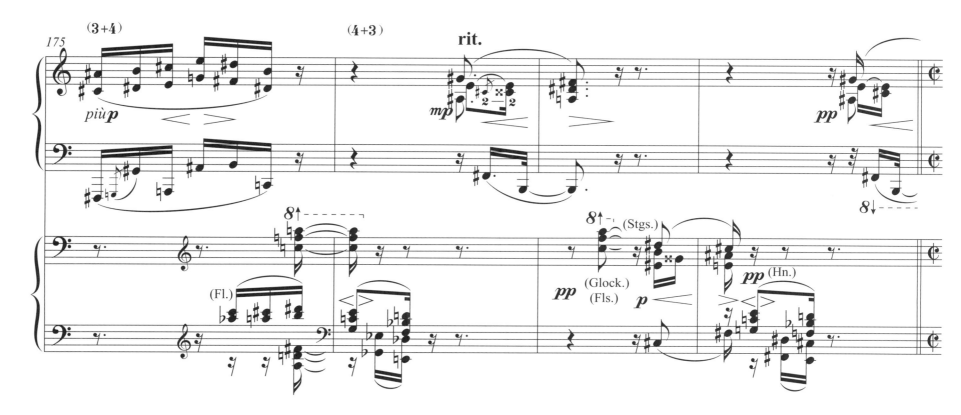

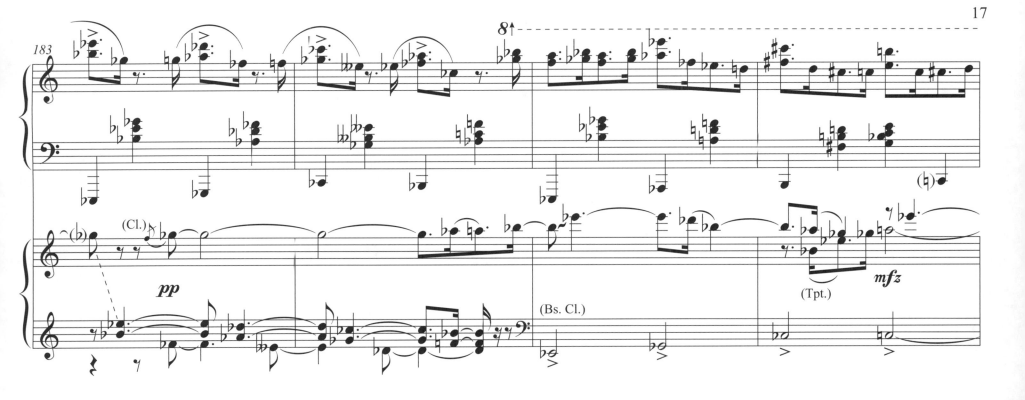

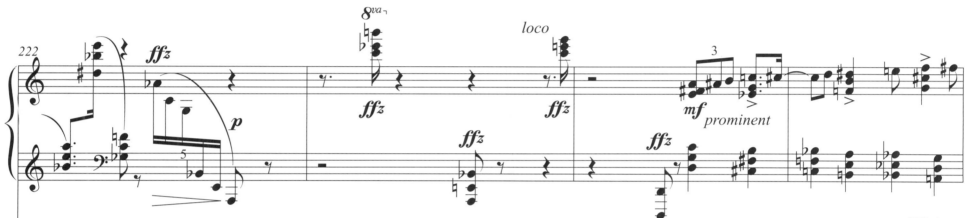

✱ cluster, including all chromatic notes within interval

Tempo I (♩=54); grandly

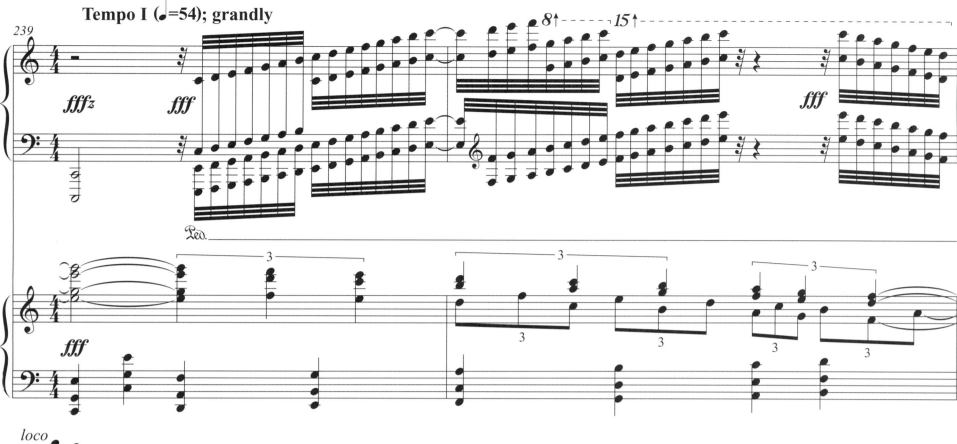

l.v. to downbeat of m. 247

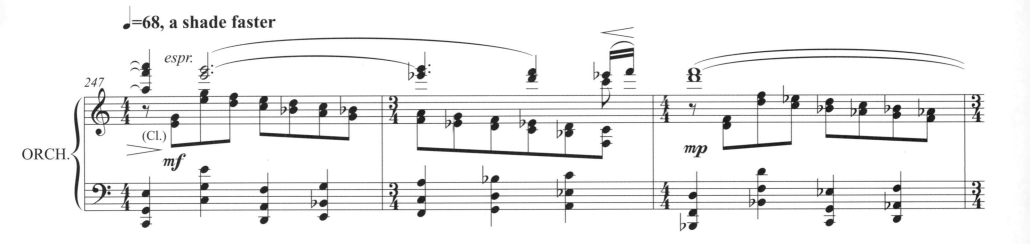

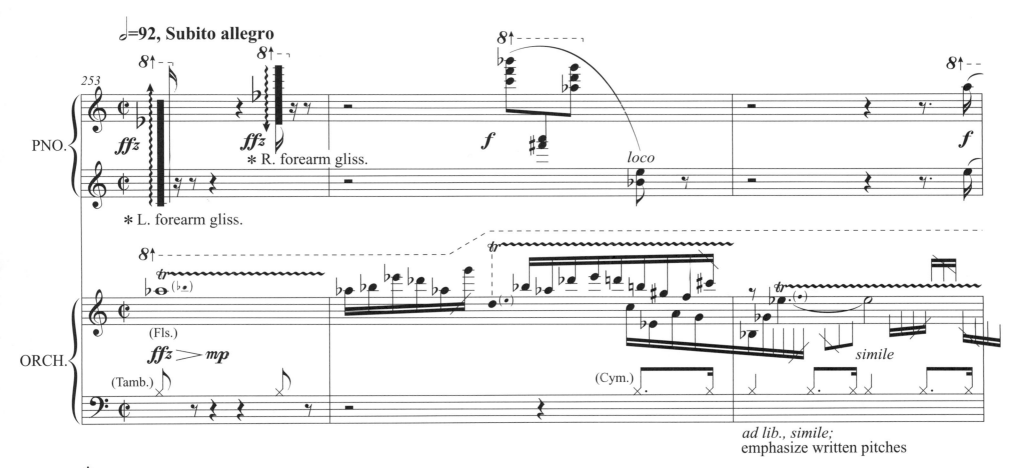

* Put elbow on keyboard and roll forearm up or down across black keys toward fingers, very quickly.

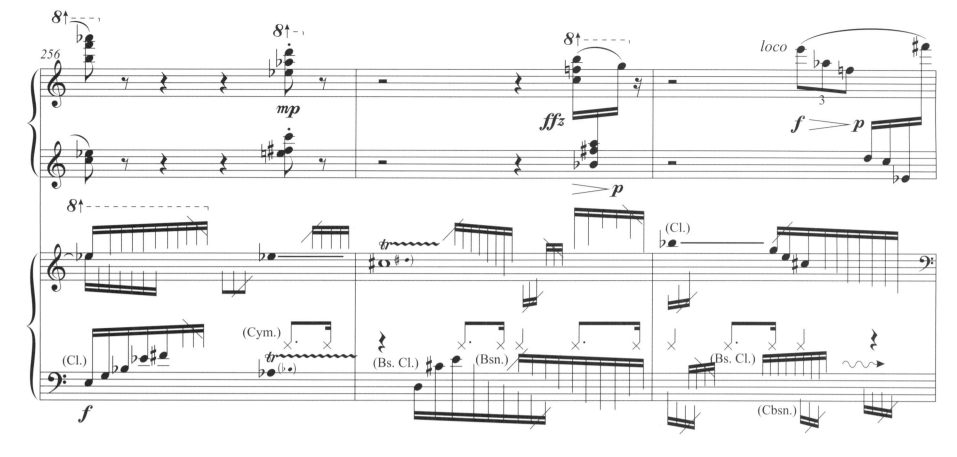

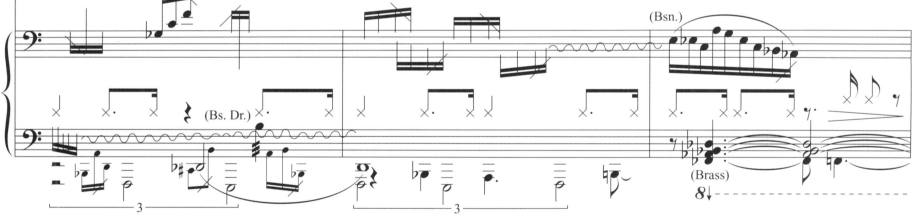

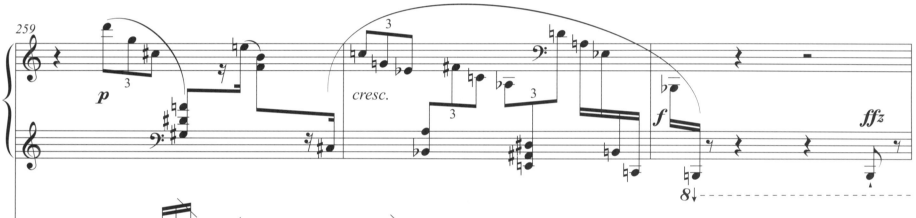

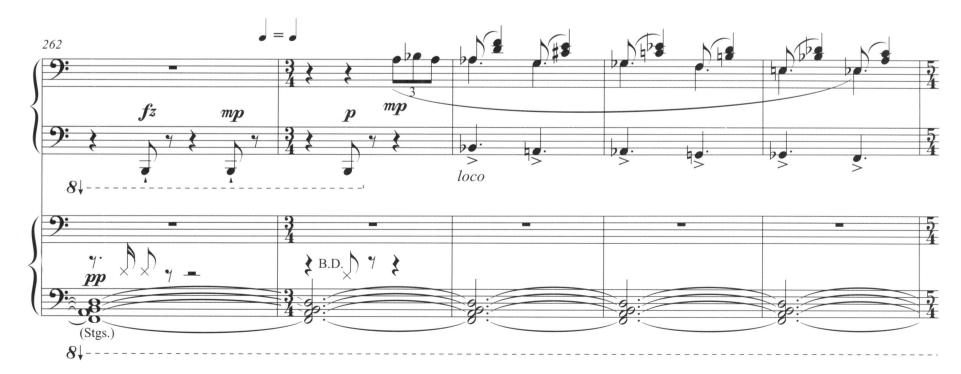

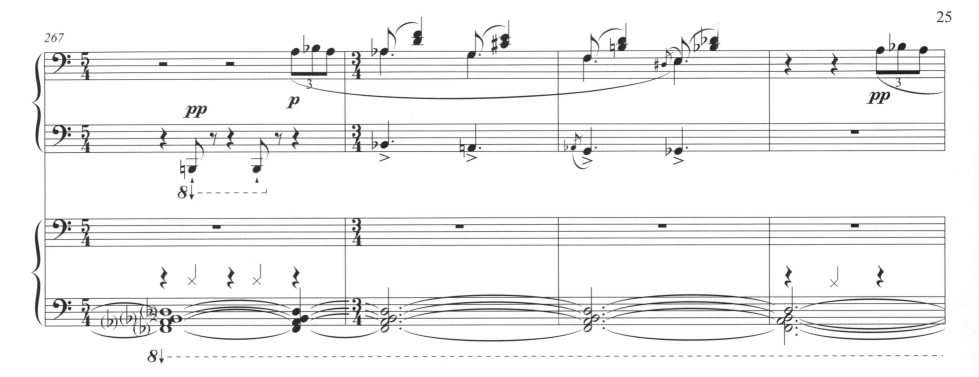

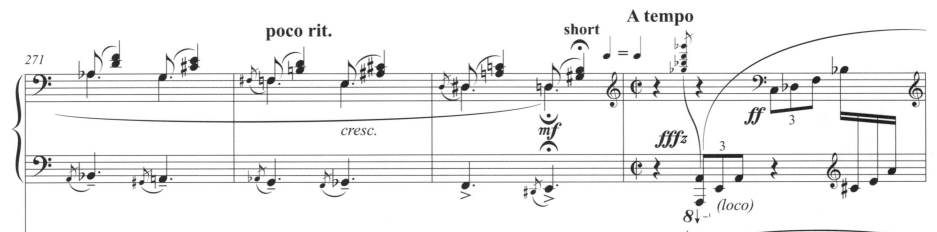

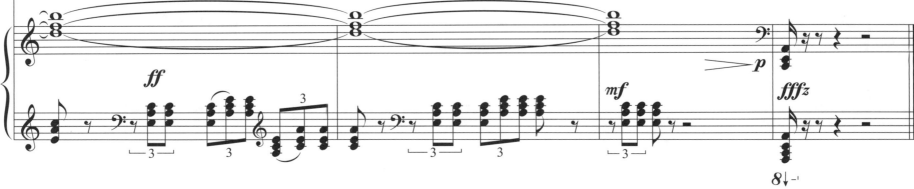

II. Regrets

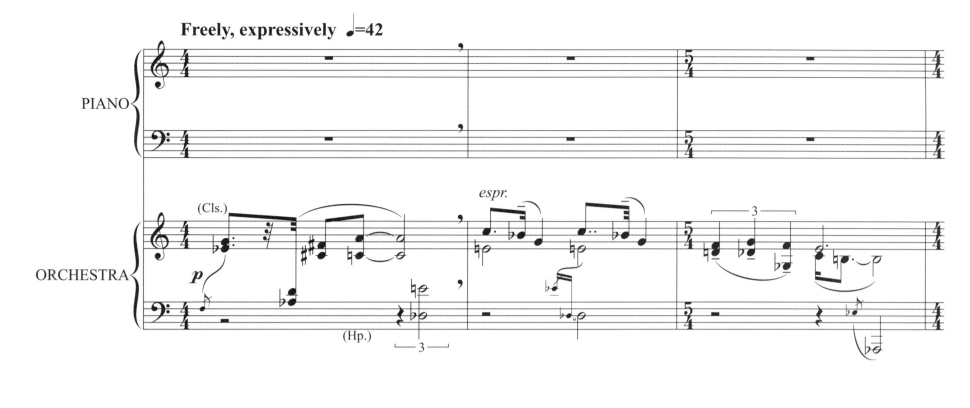

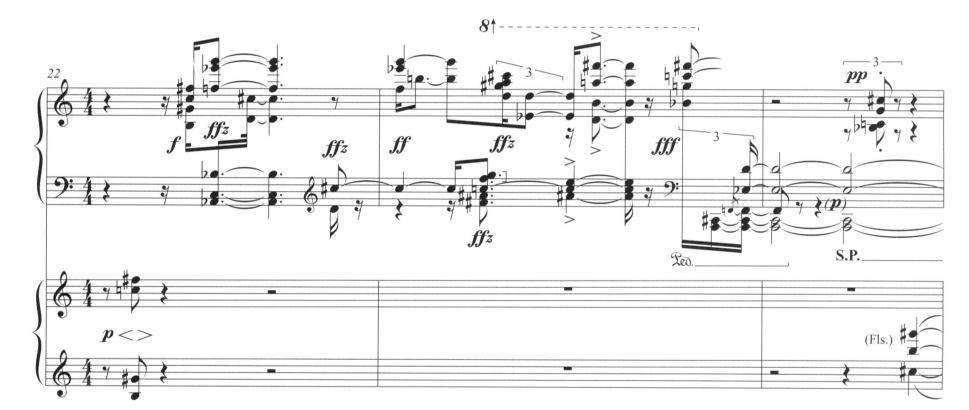

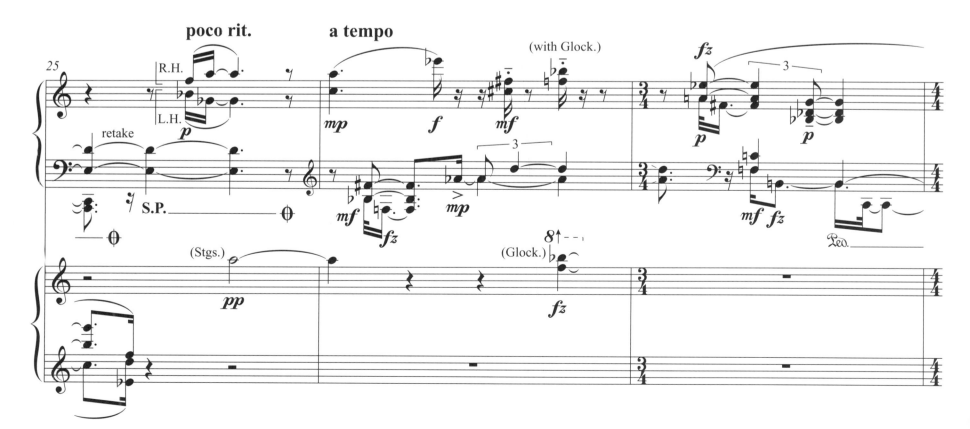

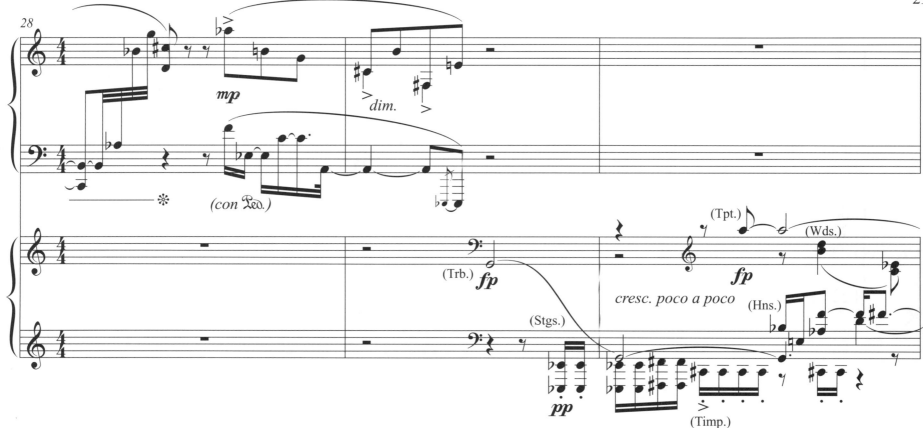

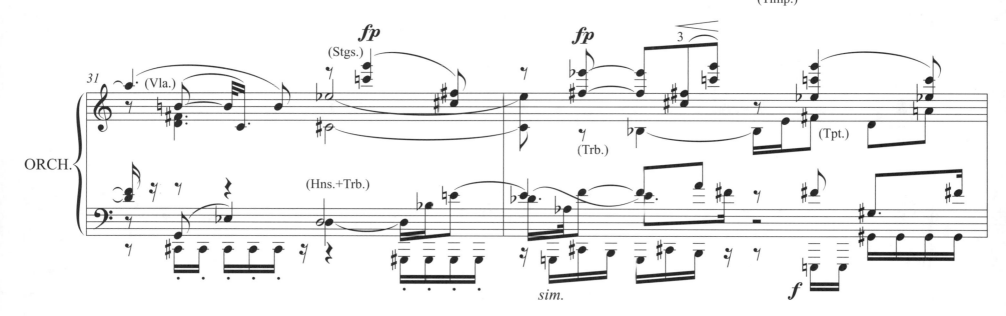

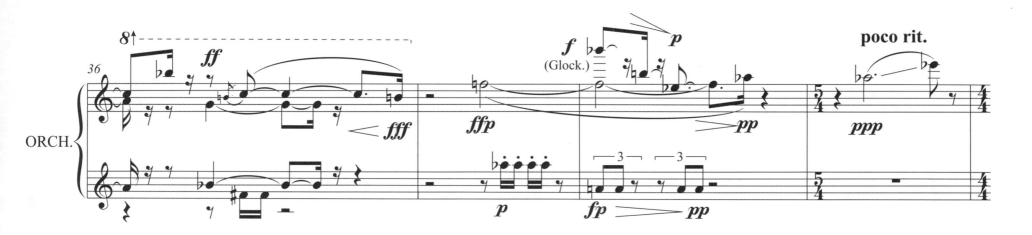

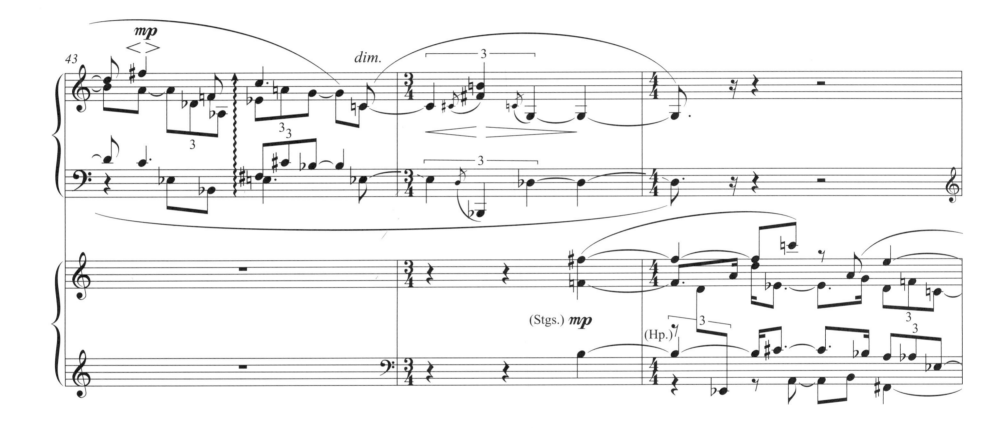

a tempo

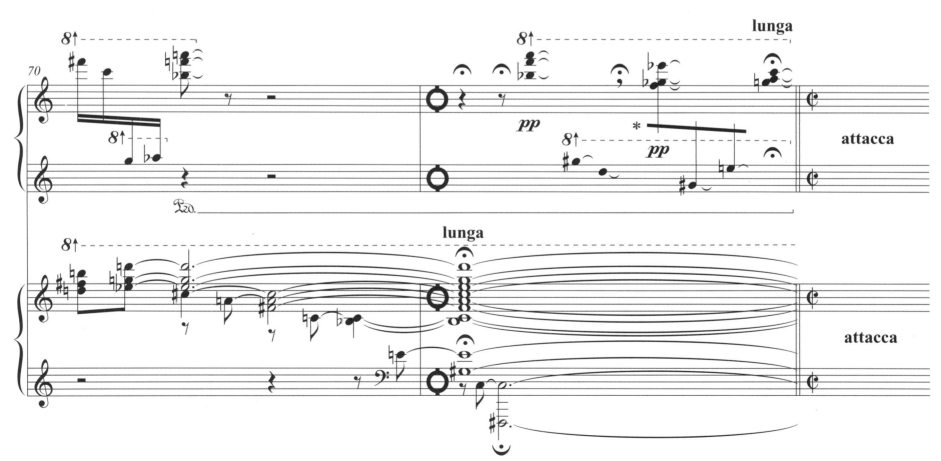

*Play loosely in rhythm.

III. Finale

Allegro molto ♩=132-138 strict tempo

PIANO

ORCHESTRA

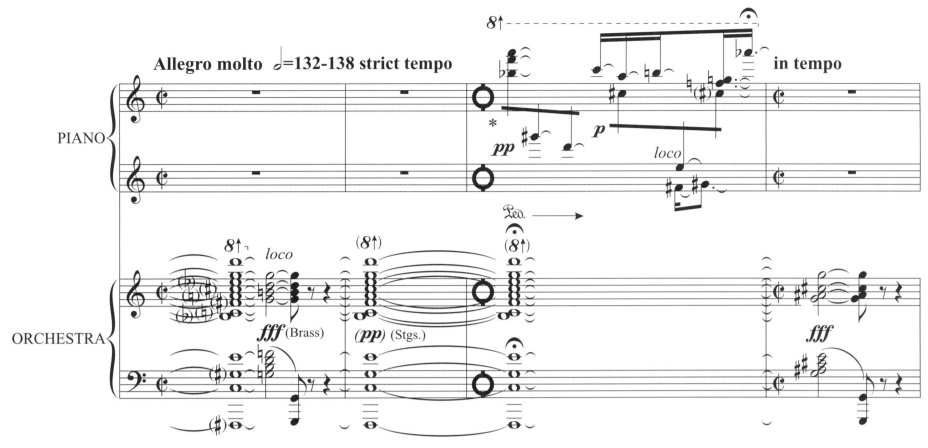

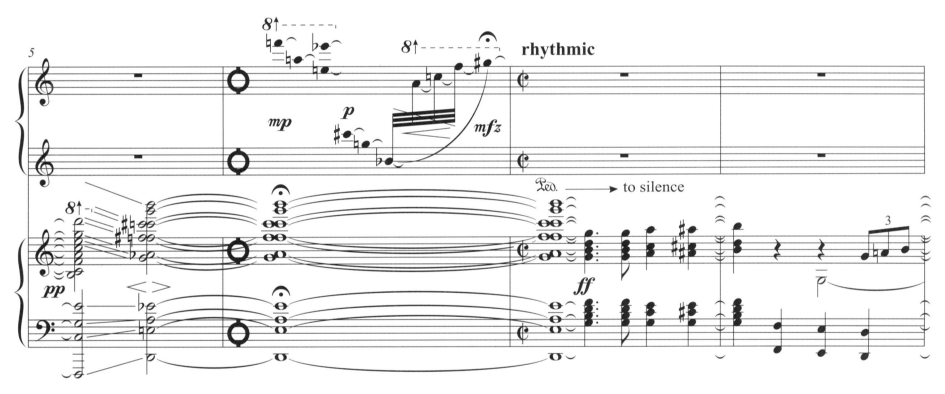

* See previous page.

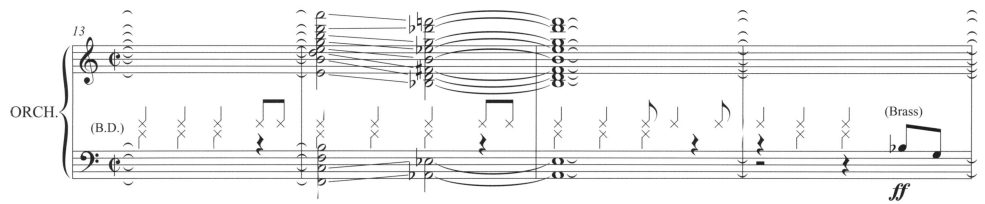

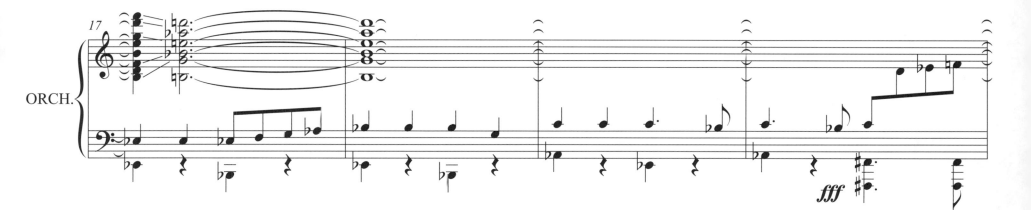

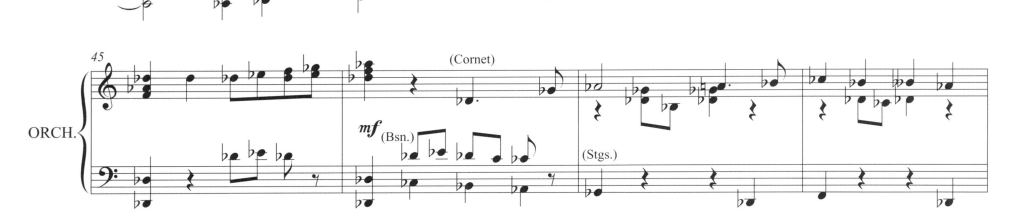

cresc. ed accel.

Presto possibile ♩=144

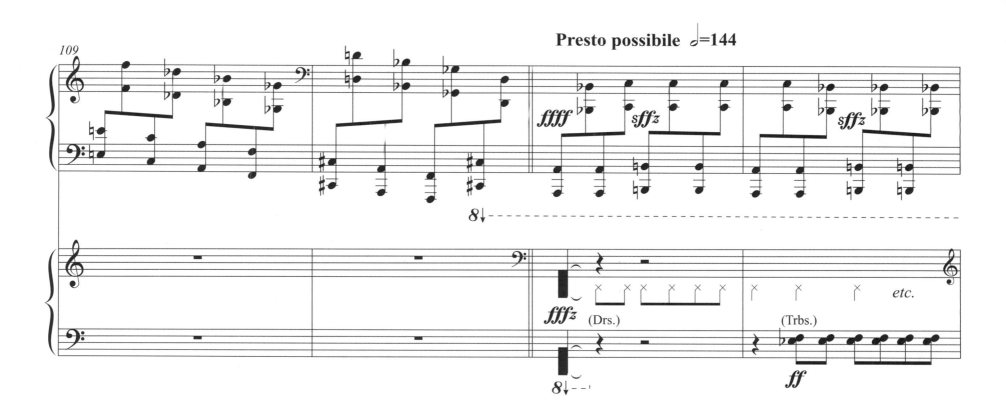

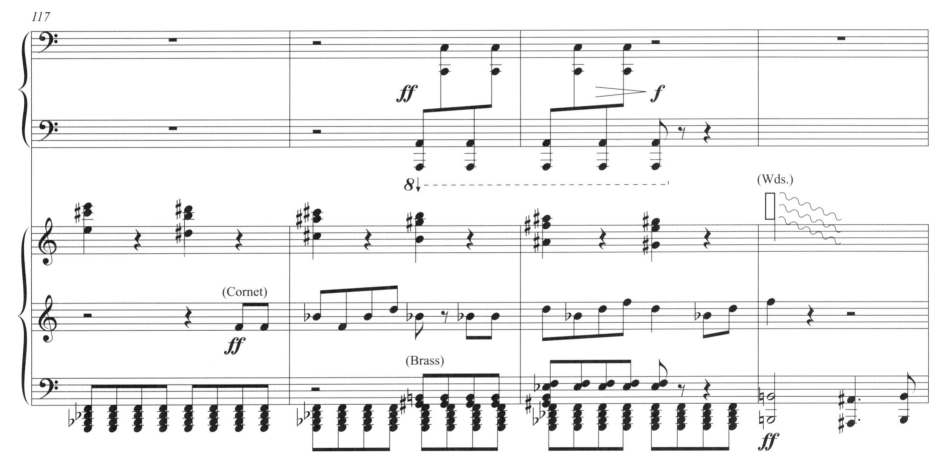

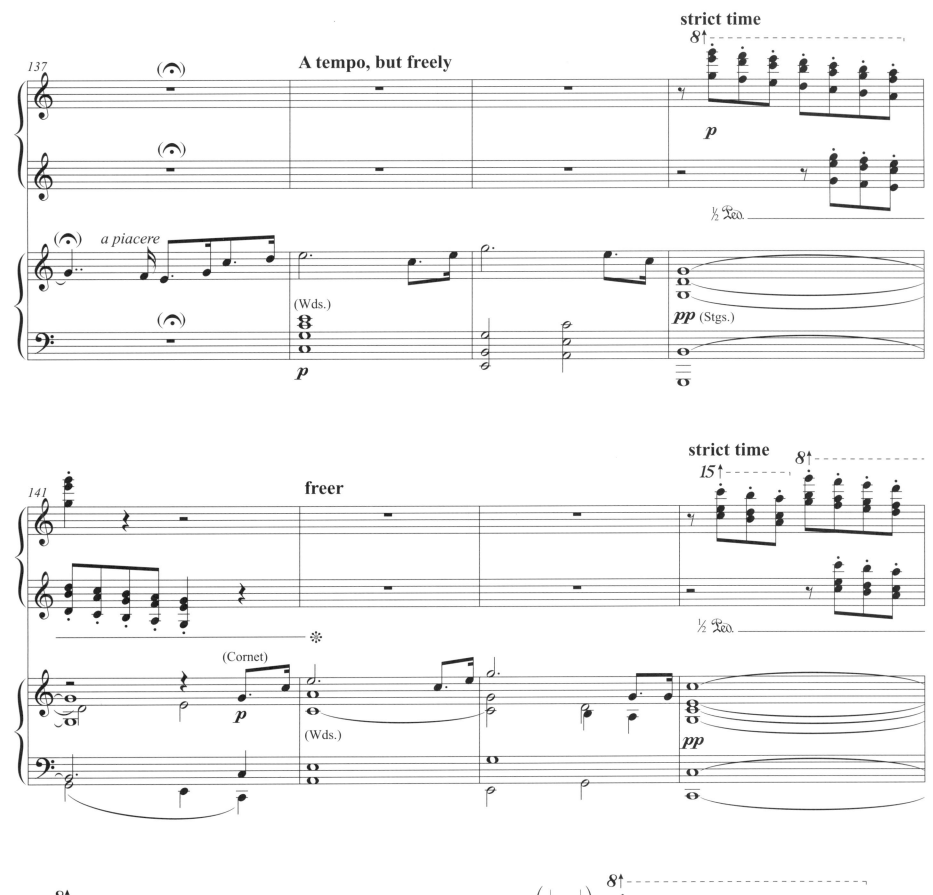

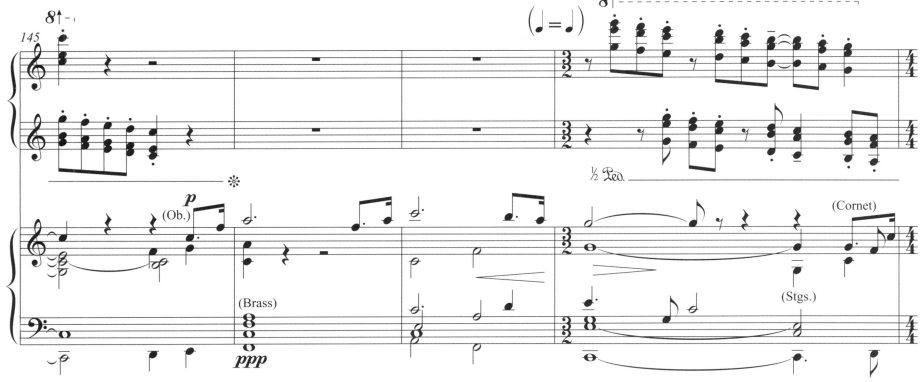

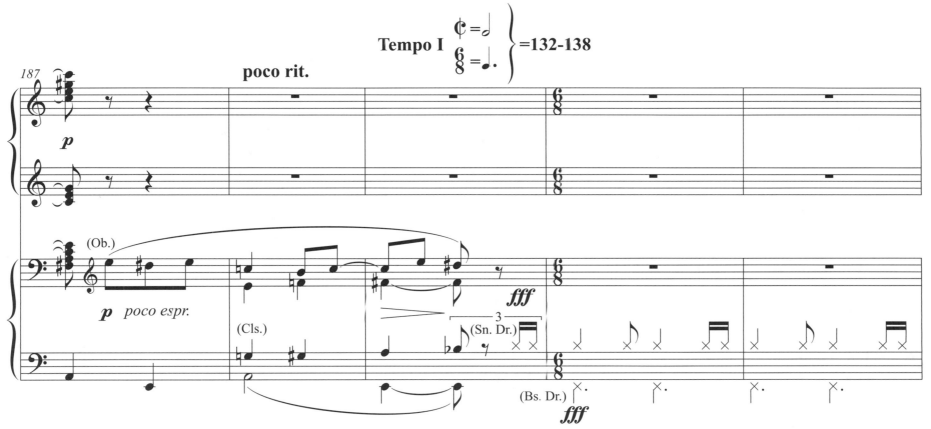

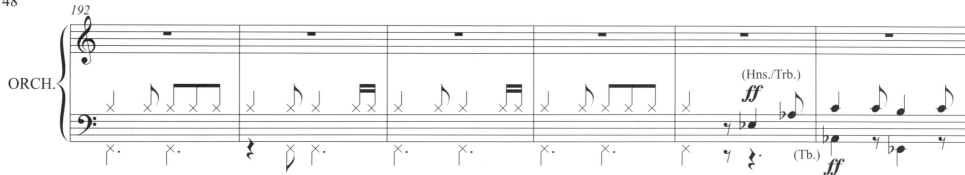

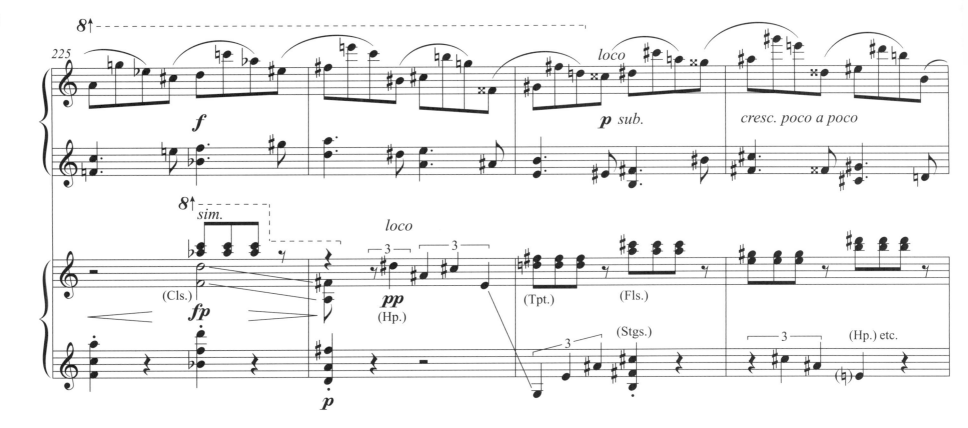

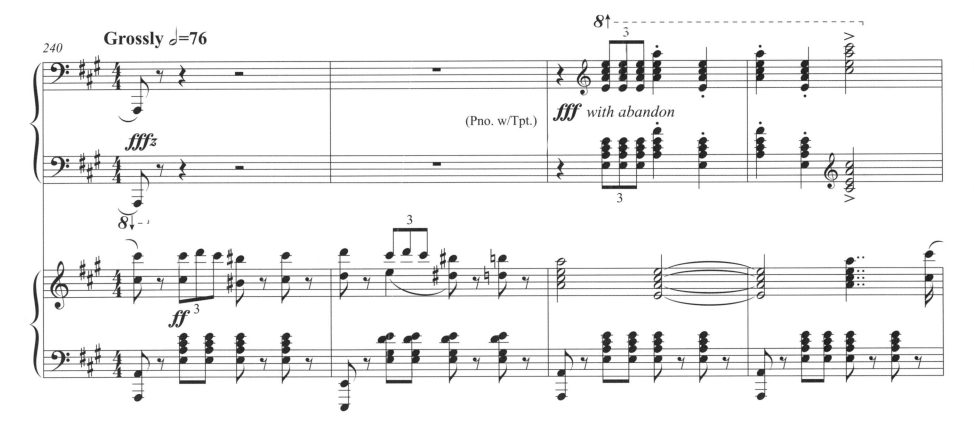

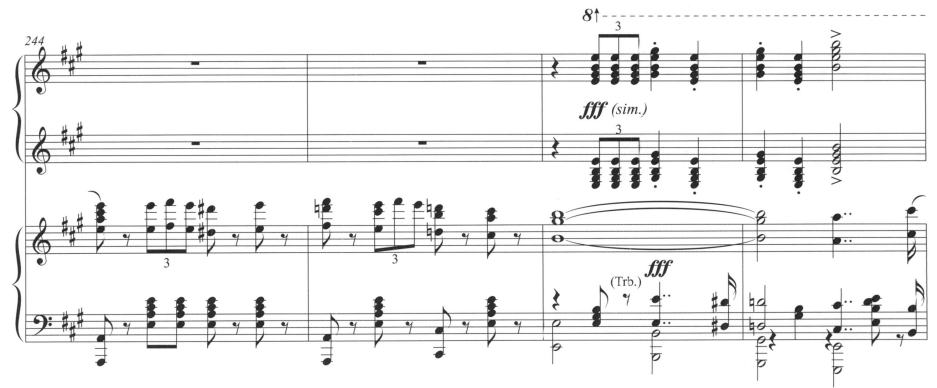

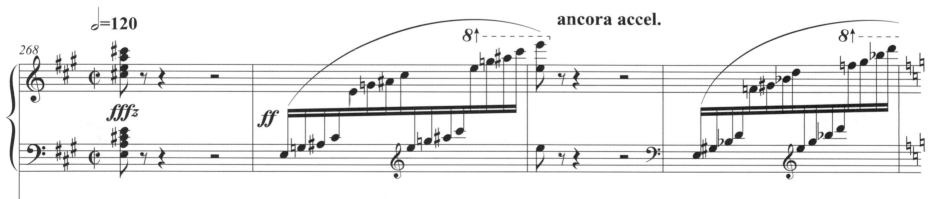

In 1

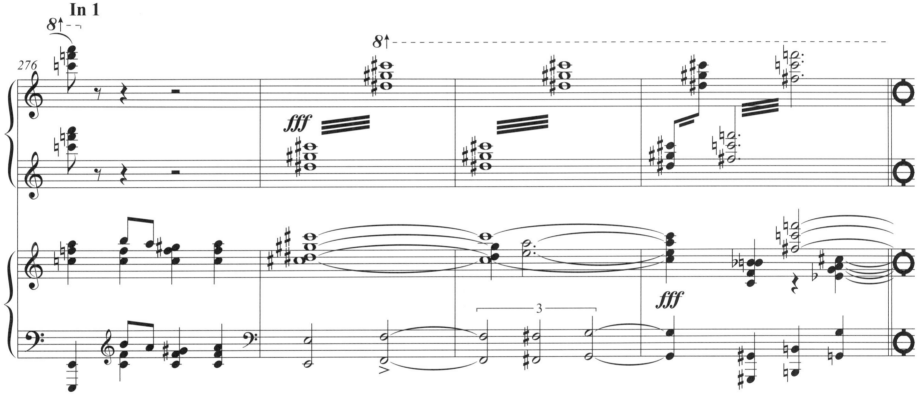

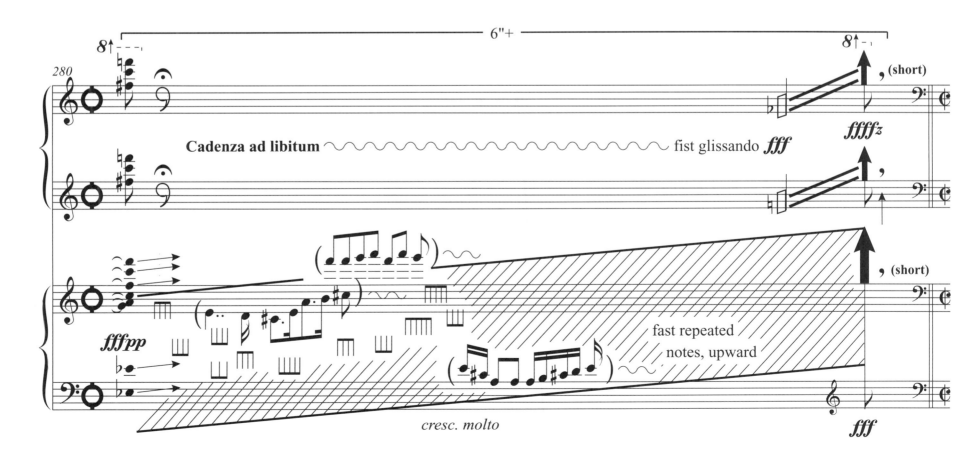

Jan. 2, 1976
Ann Arbor,
Michigan